THIS IS

CHURCH

Where **U** fit in

By

Kymone Hinds

THIS IS THE CHURCH
Published by
Watersprings Media House
Olive Branch, MS 38654
www.waterspringsmedia.com
Contact publisher for bulk orders and permission requests.

Printed in the United States of America.

ISBN-10: 0-9988249-2-5
ISBN-13: 978-0-9988249-2-5

DEDICATION

To my parents - Hollis & Anthia Hinds - who taught me so much about life. One of the most valuable lessons you taught me was to love God and love His church. Thank you!

To my brothers, Shaka & Osei and their families - I admire you both in ways I cannot explain. May you love God and serve Him with all your heart.

To my wife, Kerine, who is the greatest support any man could ask for. It's amazing how much you do with such grace. I love you! You are the real MVP!

To my children, Jaden, Janiah & Joelle, who inspire me. I am proud of the heart you each have for God. My passion is for you to find your place in God's plan.

ACKNOWLEDGEMENTS

Front Cover Design - Ornan Anthony, OA Blueprints

Photography - Marcus D. Porter, Kreative Marcs Media

Editorial - Lester & Anita Collins

REVIEWS

"Kymone has skillfully challenged our understanding of the what church is. Each chapter calls for reexamination of traditional views of the church in order to embrace the timeless principles set forth in the Scriptures. I love the church, but this book has made me love and appreciate it even more!"

Myron Edmonds, DMin., Lead Pastor Grace Community Adventist Church

"Kymone Hinds invites anyone who may be discontented with church as they know or remember to examine, explore and envision what church was meant to be."

Dilys Brooks, Associate Chaplain, Loma Linda University

"Kymone Hinds is real, but different. He doesn't run with the typical ministry herd. He leads them. Besides being a leader by example, and a community-involved pastor, Hinds' ability to take complex spiritual concerns and present them in bite-size simplicity is a rare gift. *This Is Church* is simplistic substance for the soul."

Minister Ronnie Vanderhorst, CoFounder, Prepare Our Youth, Inc.

"The message of this book is not only insightful but necessary! Hinds bridges the gap between complex and practical and wraps the meaning of the church in a way that's engaging for every reader."

Karyle Barnes Jr., Bible Teacher, Auburn Adventist Academy

"I respect Kymone Hinds. He goes against the grain in his book "This is ChURch: Where You Fit In" and lays out kingdom principles that are essential to getting it right. I appreciate Kymone's refreshing tone like a coach coming alongside a church which, like the people in it, doesn't have it all together. The love of God and his people shines through this helpful power packed book."

Peyton Jones – Author of *Reaching the Unreached: Becoming Raiders of the Lost Art* and Church Planting Trainer for NAMB, Co-host of The Church Planter Podcast

CONTENTS

I fell in love with the church at a young age. I still remember the day my parents took my brother and I into a building to a worship gathering. I was 5 years old at the time and this whole experience was weird and different for me. I did not know when to stand and when to sit. I did not know any of the songs they were singing or the words they recited from memory so easily. We did not have dressed up clothes like everyone else. And there were other things (play and TV) I wanted to do with my time.

I cannot remember much of what I heard back then. Much of what was said was over my head. What I do remember and what I fell in love with was the people and the relationships we formed with them. They barely knew us but soon they were inviting us to their homes to eat. We went places together and did things, almost as if we were family. Come to think of it, those people were my family.

Today, the church isn't thought of as positively as I described. I understand that. There have been a lot of abuses done in the name of the church. Many have been the victims of "church hurt." Maybe some of you reading this have been hurt deeply. My heart goes out to you and you have my deepest apologies on behalf of the church.

As you read this book I invite you to rediscover what church is and what it was originally intended to be. I invite you to see the power of it, the purpose of it and the plan for it. More than that, I invite you to see yourself in it. Where do you fit in? I want you to see how what the church is relates to what you have been created to be.

So, come with me on this journey as I introduce to some and reintroduce to others something I fell in love with a long time ago - This is chURch!

CHAPTER 1

A Case of Mistaken Identity

One day, a CNN reporter was on assignment to capture shots of a wild fire. On that same day, new pilots were in training. The reporter hurried to make arrangements for a flight out. He called the airport to charter a plane and was told a small plane would be waiting for him.

When he arrived at the airport, he saw a small plane warming up outside the hanger. He jumped into the plane and yelled to the pilot, "Let's go!"

Once in the air, the reporter shouted out instructions.

"Fly low so I can get the hills on fire! Get down into the valley." The pilot was confused.

"Why?" he asked. *"Because I am a camera man for CNN and I need to get close up shots."* The pilot was strangely silent for a while. Then he managed to reply. *"So, you're telling me you're not my flight instructor."*

A case of mistaken identity.

Mistaken identity is actually not a funny thing. If you have ever been the victim of identity theft you know that someone taking your identity is not funny. If someone has ever posed as or presented themselves as you, you know it is not a laughing matter.

When your identity is compromised, people begin to judge you based not on who you are or what you've done. You are judged based on the actions of the impostor, and who they are rubs off on you. Expectations and limitations are placed on you based on what they have done.

It could cost you lots of time and money. Bills that they ran up that you would have to clear up or even pay for. There are letters you have to write to restore your name and reputation. All this work needs to be done in order to restore your identity.

I believe the church has been the victim of mistaken identity. The church for a long time has been mischaracterized and misunderstood. It's been evaluated and judged based on false identification.

When we hear the word "church", different images, definitions, and thoughts come to mind. But the "church" is really not what we think.

For most of us, "church" is a building. It's a place we come to. It's a location where we center our religious life (or activity). It may look traditional with a steeple, or be a modern facility, but it's still a "place." It's a *where*.

We ask each other the question, "Where are you going today?" "To church," is the answer.

We have mistaken the church for a building. But that's not biblical.

The danger with thinking of church as a building is that it means I can live two separate lives. I do my religious activities at "church". I pray, read my Bible, and worship at "church." But when I get out of "church" I return back to my life.

It allows us to live one life within the building, and our other life is lived disconnected from what happens in that building.

Someone put it this way, "If church is a place you come to, then it's a place you leave." That's the first mistaken identity of what the church is.

The second one, and this is one that many of us make, is we have mistaken the church for an event. It's something that happens once a week for a few hours. It's an experience that's supposed to fill us, thrill us, lift us up, and make us shout. And that's what many people understand church to be.

So, because we look at church as an event, we ask each other, "How was church?" In answer to that we might say, "we had church today." This means the person enjoyed themselves and felt encouraged or lifted by the event that took place. Conversely, it may be said, "church was boring," or "I didn't get anything from church today."

What we have done is mistaken a worship gathering for the church. We have made church an *experience* we have.

The church is not an "event."

You may be saying to yourself, "this is no big deal." We may even try to justify our wrong use of words...after all it's just words. But words have power, and the way we use them shapes our minds, our expectations, and the way we approach and evaluate the church.

Words carry meaning and form our mindset and determine our expectations. The words we use and the ways we use them are important. And, if we keep making the church something that it is not–mistaken identity–it can have disastrous effects...in fact, it already has.

Here is the concern. If we mistake the building or the worship gathering for the church, we will approach the church as consumers. We will look at the church as a consumer product. The truth is, most people think of church that way. We have a 'what's in it for me' mentality.

It's something we expect to *serve us*. If we are honest with ourselves, the number one thing we wonder about when we think of church is, "Will I get something out of it today?" Because church is an event at a place.

It's so subtle and simple; everyone does it, and that's a lot of why we do what we do. It's ingrained in us. To even talk about it is uncomfortable, but let's face it - the church has been the victim of mistaken identity. So, when we hear the word church, we expect the counterfeit and not the real thing.

My contention is that many have detached from what they thought church was and not what it really is. The church has had to pay the price for the mistaken identity, and we have to recapture and rediscover what the church *is*.

DISCUSSION QUESTIONS

1.   Have you ever been mistaken for someone or had someone else mistaken for you? Have you or anyone you know been a victim of identity theft? How difficult was that for you or them?

2.   When you heard the word church what did you think about before reading this chapter? How did that affect how you approached the church?

CHAPTER 2

Formed and Fueled

Vince Lombardi, the late, great coach of the Green Bay Packers football team, had a ritual that he stood up and performed in front of his team every year. Lombardi was so prolific and successful that the National Football League (NFL) championship trophy was named after him. But his speech before his team at the beginning of each season seemed so elementary. Lombardi would hold up a football and say to his team "Men, this is a football." I know you may be scratching your head too. After all, these players had probably been holding one of those oblong objects from the moment they knew how to walk. "This is not very insightful, coach," they may have said.

His point was that every year the team needed to be reminded of the basics. With all the focus on strategy and schemes, the basic building block of the game of football was the *football*. The team that won was the one that moved the ball and stopped the other from doing so.

As we talk about what the church is, let's go back to the basics of it. Let's be reintroduced to the real church. This diagram will help us explore what the church is and its relationships.

You cannot fully describe someone without taking into account their relationships. If you were to describe me, you might say that I am a Black man who works as a pastor. You might say that I am relatively tall. But that doesn't fully tell who I am.

I am a husband, a father, a son, a brother, a friend. You can describe me based on what I do, but also based on my relationships. And that's what we will do with the church.

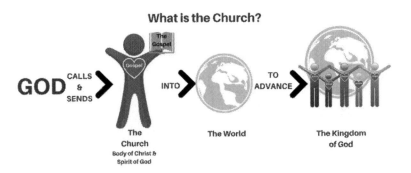

Our diagram shows the following about the church:

• The church is the *body of Christ* filled with the Spirit of God.

• The church is *called* and *sent* by God with the gospel *into the world* to advance the Kingdom of God.

Over the next few chapters, we will take a look at these elements and their relationship to what the church is. In this chapter, we will look at the aspect of the church as the body of Christ filled with the Spirit of God. Here is what we understand about the church and how that relates to us: The Church is Formed by God.

1 Corinthians 12, talks about the church being the Body of Christ and it goes on to explain what that means. It tells us that the church is a collection of people that have been brought together by God. God is the one that has planned it. God is the one that has molded us together. Verse 18 says, "But as it is, God arranged the members in the body, each one of them as He chose."

The church is made up of people, but not just people who sit together in a building for a couple hours each week to have an experience. No, the church is knitted and bonded and bound together. We are joined together in relationship with one another and are called a body by God Himself. You can't go off alone and do your thing. You can't be passive and a spectator in what the body is doing because a body is a unit.

There is a fallacy that doing exercises in one particular part of your body will cause you to lose weight in that part. So, you have people who will do a whole bunch of sit ups to reduce their mid-section. But, they don't realize that the body functions as a unit. To lose weight in your stomach you exercise your whole body.

God describes the church as a body of people together. It's not a building. It's a *body*. One of the things that means is that if you are a part of the church, God is the one that has placed you as a part of this body. You are not a part of the body by accident. You have a role and a function. You are a part of the body.

We also need to realize that as God brings people in the church, they are fashioned by God into the same body. Even those who we may be at odds with, God has molded them into His church.

THE CHURCH IS FUELED BY GOD

Acts 1:8 – *"But you will receive power when the Holy Spirit has come upon you, and you will be my witnesses in Jerusalem and Judea and Samaria and to the end of the earth."*

In this text, Jesus is addressing the body of believers that he has formed, telling them that they will get power. The power for the church to do what God has called her to do comes from the Holy Spirit. The Spirit of God enables the church to do its mission.

When we read the book of Acts, we see the church exercising power because of the presence of the Holy Spirit. The church is active and in motion. The church is so powerful because it is demonstrating the same formula at work that God used when He formed the first man.

In Genesis 2:7, God formed the body of man. Then God breathed in his nostrils the breath of life. The word used in Genesis for breath is the same as Spirit.

BODY + SPIRIT = LIVING SOUL

God has formed another body! It's this thing called the church. It's the Body of Christ. However, in John 20:22, we find that Jesus does something powerful with the body that he has been forming. The Bible says, "*And when he said this, he breathed on them and said, 'Receive the Holy Spirit'.*"

BODY OF CHRIST + SPIRIT OF GOD =LIVING CHURCH

And that's what the church is–it's a people formed by God together in a relationship bond that is like a body. God infuses that body of people with the power of His Holy Spirit so they can have life.

The Church & The Gospel

The Church
Body of Christ &
Spirit of God

DISCUSSION QUESTIONS

1. Have you found your unique role in the body? If you could describe it as a body part what would it be?

2. How does knowing God formed the body affect the way you look at dealing with difficult people in the church?

CHAPTER 3

Have A Heart

S*tart with Why* is the bestselling book by Simon
Sinek. In it he shares that great leaders inspire
action not by beginning with the how and the what
of the activity or plan. Great leaders, he says, get people
to buy into the "why" - the reason behind the mission.
Why you do what you do. It is fascinating to study
people in whatever field of life and see what drives them
and makes them get out of bed in the morning and
pursue their goals. This is the heart of who they are.

Have you ever wondered what the heart of the church
is? What is the why behind this body of Christ, that is
powered by the Spirit of God? What should be the
motivating factor behind our actions and our plans?
What is at the heart of the church?

Although at times we may have various motives as
churches for our activity such as paying the bills,
increasing our membership roll and giving the
appearance of success, the Bible seems to give a different
"why" behind what we do. In 2 Corinthians 5:17-21, the
author, Paul shares a compelling why and that is the
GOSPEL. The reason he gives for all the gathering and
sharing and serving and helping is the gospel.

Now what is the gospel? I'm glad you asked. The gospel simply is: God was in Christ, reconciling the world to himself, no longer counting people's sins against them. And He gave us this wonderful message of reconciliation. 2 Cor 5:19 (NLT).

The Bible starts off in Genesis with the story of a perfect God making a perfect man to live in a perfect world in a perfect relationship with Him. But then into this perfection comes this strange, mysterious alien concept called sin. Sin separates man from God. It breaks the connection, and the story of humanity is the story of humans trying to deal with that disconnection.

Some try to ignore it and pretend there's nothing missing. But that doesn't deal with the emptiness that is there due to the broken relationship. Some try to reconnect it by bringing God down to their level. Making God just like them. Making God so low that they can reach Him. But that doesn't fix the broken relationship.

Then some try to reconnect by their own efforts. Some try to work real hard, and do a lot of ceremonies and symbols and live so good that their good deeds serve as rungs on a ladder. A ladder they use to climb up to reconnect them back to God. But everyone who has tried that realizes that our ladders are too short and they are leaning against an imaginary wall. Our good works and good deeds don't reconnect a broken relationship.

So, since there needs to be a perfect person to reconnect man back to God and no man was ever and could ever be good enough, God became man. God was in Christ reconciling the world unto Himself. Jesus came down to hold the live wire, that had been cut. God through Christ reconnects man to God holding the live wire and the connection was restored. God becomes a man so that He could do for man what man could never do for himself - He restores a broken relationship!

Because sin was the thing that caused the separation, how does God deal with the separating agent? Sin has to be dealt with. There is a wage for sin called death. The gospel says it in Romans 6:23.

The Church & The Gospel

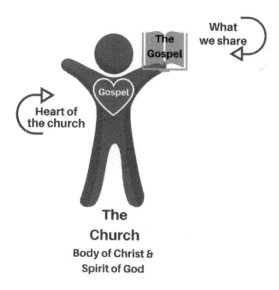

THE GOSPEL

Christ reconnects man back to God. The broken relationship is restored. God puts the punishment on Christ and we get the benefits he has earned. That's the GOSPEL.

So how does that relate to the church? What does that story of reconnection of a broken relationship have to do with the church? Everything!

The gospel is the heart of the church. It's the reason we do what we do. 2 Corinthians 5:14 - 15 says it so well,

"For the love of Christ controls us, because we have concluded this: That one has died for all, therefore all have died and He died for all, that those who live might no longer live for themselves but for him who for their sake died and was raised."

The love of Christ is what makes us do what we do. Because of what He did for us, we live for Him. What we do isn't about what we want, it's about what He wants. The reason why we, the church, do what we do is because of what God has done in us. The church is reconciled people living out the freedom of that reconciliation.

We do everything because of what He did. The reason we as the church worship is because of what Christ did. The reason we serve one another is because of what Christ did. The reason we give our time, our talent, and our treasure, is because of what Christ did. The reason we do all we do, give all we give, go where we go, is because of what Jesus did. The love of Christ is our why!

It's dangerous for us as to be motivated by anything else. If we make anything else the primary motivation for doing what we are doing it will fail. If we try to make fear the reason we try to make the church move it may work for a while, but it doesn't change our heart and it will eventually stop working. If we are motivated by guilt, it will only work for a while. Even being driven by some blessing we want to acquire may work, but only for a while. All of these, lead to misery instead of joy in service. The only motivation that changes the heart is the gospel of Jesus Christ.

LET IT OVERFLOW

They tell us that what's inside your heart will come out. It will come out in what you say, in your expressions. If something has made a deep, lasting impact on you, it will flow out of you. The gospel will flow out of the church, you and me, to those we come in contact with. We will tell it and show it by our words and our actions. We can't help but live out 2 Corinthians 5:20,

"Therefore, we are ambassadors for Christ, God making his appeal through us. We implore you on behalf of Christ, be reconciled to God."

God in Christ reconciled the world to Himself. When we get an understanding of that and it rocks our heart and it fires us up as the church then we 'run tell dat.' Our job is to be agents of reconciliation and tell the world that reconciliation has happened.

We carry one message to the world. That message is BE reconciled to God. That's different from the message people hear all around them. It's different than anything they've ever believed before because all of life says, GET reconciled to God. Everything says, you've got issues and God is angry with you because of your issues and so you have got to get it right before you come to God. And in the midst of a world that says "Get" reconciled to God,

He has sent the church with the message "BE" reconciled to God. It's not something you work to achieve. It's not something you have to earn. It's a new reality that has been worked out for you. The reconciliation has already taken place between God and man. And God is inviting people to live out that new reality. God is not out to get you. Reconciliation has already taken place. Now come accept it. Come live like it. Come receive it. That's our why - THE GOSPEL!

DISCUSSION QUESTIONS

1. What was your understanding of the gospel before reading this chapter? How did that understanding affect the way you lived?

2. What is the difference between "Get Reconciled" and "Be Reconciled"? How does that change the way you approach people you want to share the gospel with?

CHAPTER 4

Love/Hate

A modern philosopher once said, "You can't hate what you didn't once love." Her contention is that love and hate are the extremes of the same emotion. To hate is a commitment. This philosopher and scholar says that in order to hate something, you have to have had some emotional tie to it at first. In order to hate something, you could not have been indifferent to it. Then those feelings turn on its head from a strong positive to a strong negative feeling.

It's interesting that for many of us, we can have a love/hate relationship with the same thing or same person, at the same time. We can have a strong affinity for something but have a strong dislike for it at the same time. Simple case in point: My body has a love/hate relationship with chocolate. My taste buds love it; my tummy hates it. Love/hate relationship.

As we discuss the church and the world, it's clear that there is a love/hate relationship going on. When we examine how the church has been called and sent into the world, we find a tension. There is a love/ hate relationship between the church and the world. If we are not careful, we can be confused about our role and function. We can be confused as to how to relate, interact or connect with the world around us.

John 3:16 & 17 tells us: *"For God so loved the world, that he gave his only Son, that whoever believes in Him should not perish but have eternal life. For God did not send His Son into the world to condemn the world, but in order that the world might be saved through Him."*

It is clear that God loves the world and God sends His Son into the world. We should love what God loves. So, we are to love the world. However, when it talks about the world, it is talking about people – the people of the world. God loves the people of the world.

But 1 John 2:15-17 (same author, by the way) says:

"Do not love the world or the things in the world. If anyone loves the world, the love of the Father is not in him. For all that is in the world – the desires of the flesh and the desires of the eyes and the pride of life – is not from the Father, but is from the world. And the world is passing away along with its desires, but whoever does the will of God abides forever."

All that is in the world is referring to things. It's talking about the ideals and values. It's talking about ideology of the world. It explains its meaning: The lust of the flesh, the lust of the eyes and the pride of life.

God loves the world so much that He sent His Son to die for it. We should love what God loves. But on the other hand, don't love the world! If you love the world, the love of the Father isn't in you.

Love the world. Hate the world. Love/hate relationship. Let's stay on this a bit more...

2 Corinthians 6:17 in the NKJV says:

"Therefore, come out from among them and be separate, says the Lord. Do not touch what is unclean, and I will receive you."

Come out from the world. But, then Mark 16:15 says: And He said to them,

"Go into all the world and preach the gospel to every creature."

Go into the world, come out from the world.

Do you catch the tension? Do you feel the strain? Are you seeing this awkward relationship?

God calls us to love the world. God calls us to hate the world. We can keep going text after text. One that says, I'm sending you into the world. Another says, Come out from the world.

God has a heart and a love for the world. You are to hate the world. The world will hate you. It's a love/hate relationship. It can be confusing. We like either/or. We like black or white. We want to know yes or no. But in this case, this tension does not go away. It's not an either/or. It's a both/and.

We love the world AND hate the world at the same time. The key for the church is to figure out how to love the world and hate the world at the same time.

The foundational principle of worldliness is selfishness. And the Bible says, hate that: The world's value system.

Unfortunately, too often we do the exact opposite. We love the value system and the ideology of the world, and we live by it. But we hate the people of the world and we disengage from them.

God is calling the church to love the world – the people in the world – and God is calling the church to hate the world – the value system of the world. So how does the church accomplish this? How do we develop and maintain the right love/ hate relationship? How do we ensure we're loving the people and hating the values?

In the next chapter, we will look at the powerful reality that God uses the same thing to call us out of the world that He sends us back into the world.

DISCUSSION QUESTIONS

1. Is there anything you have or ever had a love/ hate relationship with? Which one was stronger - love or hate?

2. Have you found yourself loving the things of the world while not caring for the people of the world? What shift can you make to love the people while hating the principles of worldliness?

CHAPTER 5

Saved and Sent

I am sure that I am not the only one it has happened to. I have composed important emails to send to coworkers, my boss, people that I minister to. I put all the details that were necessary in that email and checked all of the spelling and grammar to ensure I made the best impression. And then I waited. I was waiting for a response from the other person. Waiting for an answer to my question and I did not receive it in a timely manner.

When I followed up by phone call or text, the other person informed me that they never received the email that I had spent all that time working on. Well, I did what we all do. I went into my email and looked at my outbox only to realize I never hit the sent button and that email stayed for days or hours in the draft folder. I know I am not the only one that has happened to. That email was saved but not sent. And it did not have the effect that it should have had because it never was sent.

As we discussed in the last chapter, God is calling the church to love the world – the people in the world, and to hate the world – the value system of the world. So how does the church accomplish this?

The Church & The World

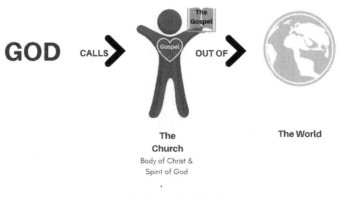

CALLED OUT

First, we recognize that God calls the church out of the world using the gospel – the good news of what Christ has done for us. Not good advice of what we should do to live a better life, but the news that because we could not do anything good, Jesus came and lived a perfect life and gave us credit for it. And that news calls us away from the value system of the world into this body God has formed that's living by a new value system.

1 Peter 2:9 says this:

"But you are a chosen race, a royal priesthood, a holy nation, a people for His own possession, that you may proclaim the excellencies of Him who called you out of darkness into his marvelous light."

The church has been called out of the world by God using the gospel, and that's how we are saved. And by the same power of the gospel, God continues to call the world out of us. That's a continuous process to form our hearts to be like His heart.

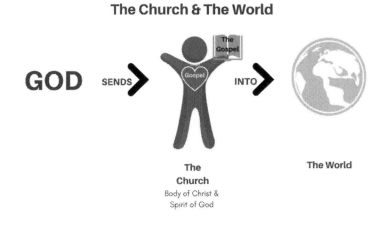

The Church & The World

GOD SENDS INTO

The
Church
Body of Christ &
Spirit of God

The World

SENT BACK

God does not only call the church out of the world, He sends the church back into the world. In John 17 we find Jesus praying for His church. He is getting ready to go to the cross and we find His longest recorded prayer. In this prayer, He prays for the church.

Let's look at verses 14 – 18, *"I have given them your word, and the world has hated them because they are not of the world, just as I am not of the world. I do not ask that you take them out of the world, but that you keep them from the evil one. They are not of the world, just as I am not of the world. Sanctify them in the truth; your word is truth. As you sent me into the world, so I have sent them into the world."*

In this prayer, Jesus is praying specifically for the church. He says the world will hate the church. He says don't take them out of the world, but keep them from the value system of the world. Sanctify them through your truth. Continue to get the worldly principles out of them. And then He says, I am sending the church back into the world.

Jesus calls us out of the world, so He can send us back into the world. He calls us away from that value system so we can go back and reach others who still live by that value system.

For God loves the people of the world so much that He chose their well-being over the safety of His Son. And He says to His church, now go reach them, go tell them.

God is a sending God. He sends the Son into the world. The Son sends the Spirit into the world. The Father, Son and the Spirit send the church into the world.

The Church & The World

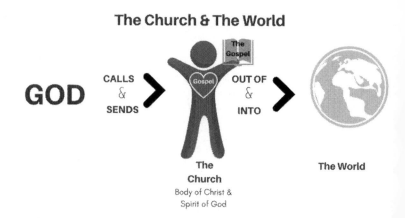

God has a mission to reach people in our world and He has called us – the church – to be a part of that mission. And many of us as Christians are like that email I talked about earlier. We are saved, but we are not sent.

Each of us should embrace that, individually and collectively, God is sending us to someone to reach, serve, and share the gospel. The reason we work where we work and live where we live is because there is someone in that circle that God is sending us to.

What if we prayed and asked God to move us out of the draft folder? Ask God who He is sending you to and then determine to live life in a way that allows you to interact, build relationships and be the good news to people around you.

FIT TO GO

I started playing basketball at a local YMCA a few years ago. I was out of shape and lacked confidence in my skill. So, I was honestly playing defense on offense. I did not want to get the ball passed to me because I was afraid I would mess up. I was unfit and not confident in my ability.

And that's how I had lived before I moved here to Memphis. I lived closed off to others. I did not want God to send me to anyone.

But when I realized that because of the gospel, I am already empowered and have all I need, I learned to live openly. I live now with new eyes asking God to show me who He is sending my way. I have intentionally began to engage in activities like running with others so I can meet people in my neighborhood. I have begun reaching out to invite neighbors to family celebrations. I am equipped by the gospel to do His work. Now I want God to send me to people and send people to me.

It's time we lived saved and sent.

DISCUSSION QUESTIONS

1. In what ways are you living by the world's value system and what is God calling you out of or calling out of you?

2. Who is God sending you to be the church to and to reach for him? How can you connect with them deeper and share the gospel?

CHAPTER 6

Playing to Win

"You play to win the game...Hello."

– Herman Edwards

I
t was one of the most memorable rants in sports interview history. The head coach of the New York Jets (my football team), Herman Edwards, after a particularly difficult loss, had gotten one too many questions from reporters. It was then that he uttered the line - "You play to win the game!"

No matter what the endeavor, there is something in us that wants to know what the win is. From games on a playground, to academic pursuits, to our jobs, we want to know what success is. We want to have markers that determine whether we are hitting our target and achieving our goals. We have measurements to tell us if we are making progress. We want to know what the win is. And you play to win the game...hello!

It is the same with the church. We have to determine what the win is for the church. We all as the church consciously or unconsciously want to know if we are winning. After we have invested our time and given our resources and used our talents with a group of people, we want to know we have not wasted our energy or effort.

There are traditional measurements that have been used to determine success - people being baptized, budget being met, buildings being acquired or renovated and more bodies in the seats during a worship service. These are all good things and I think it is important for us to continue to encourage and track these things.

THERE MUST BE MORE

There is something in competition called a "hollow victory." It is when you win but you don't get the satisfaction from it that you thought you would. It leaves you wanting more, longing for something else to conquer. For some reading this, the markers of success for a church may seem like a "hollow victory." All of them may not excite you and there is a nagging suspicion that there must be more.

If the church is not a building and not an event, then winning cannot simply be tied to improving buildings and increasing attendance at an event. Winning has to be something else and I believe the Bible challenges us to something more. Maybe we need to shift away from seeing winning as being about the church and seeing it as being about the kingdom of God. The role of the church, every local church, is to advance the kingdom of God.

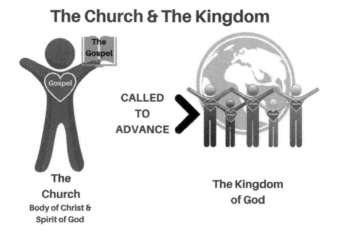

IT'S ALL ABOUT THE KINGDOM

The kingdom of God is the rule and reign of God. God has already established that kingdom here on earth. Even in the midst of brokenness and the evil in the world, God has always had a domain that He reigns over here. The role of the church is to claim wins for God's kingdom. How do we do that? Here are three ways each local body, no matter how big or small can advance the kingdom.

WINNING NEW HEARTS FOR GOD

Each local church should be seeking to take the gospel to those in their city who have not heard about the love of Jesus or accepted Him as their Lord and Savior. We each have that responsibility. Individually we are called to live as missionaries in the world, taking the Great News of the gospel to people who do not know it or may not grasp its power for them. When we do so we expand the Kingdom as hearts are submitted to God and He reigns as King over their lives.

LIVING OUT KINGDOM PRINCIPLES

Another way we advance the kingdom of God is by living out the values of the kingdom here on earth. In Matthew 20:25-28, Jesus outlines how His Kingdom would operate. It would not be modeled on the hierarchal systems of the world where the most important person sits at the top of the structure and is served. No...Jesus said, *"whoever would be great among you must be your servant."* Jesus demonstrated and taught service as a lifestyle. The church should be always seeking to serve the community, without any strings attached because when the church does, it is living out the principles of the kingdom and that in itself is a win. Anytime we serve, make a difference in the world, seek to restore brokenness or bring justice to those who have been left out, we are advancing the Kingdom of God. We may not see any tangible benefit to ourselves (and we shouldn't look for it), but we are winning.

THY KINGDOM COME

The final way that the church advances the kingdom of God is by bringing in the ultimate and visible reign of God on earth. Matthew 24:14 says it this way *"And this gospel of the kingdom will be proclaimed throughout the whole world as a testimony to all nations, and then the end will* come." *The end will come when "the kingdom of the world has become the kingdom of our Lord and of his Christ, and he shall reign forever and ever."* Revelation 11:15.

The church is called to usher in this ultimate revelation of the Kingdom of God. Right now, the Kingdom is invisible and not fully apparent in this world. But there is a day coming when it will completely takeover this world. Matthew 24:14 is clear that this will happen when the gospel is proclaimed throughout the world.

While each church can help spread the gospel where they are and serve where they are, we all cannot take the good news around the world by ourselves. This is where we need to look away from ourselves and partner with others around the world to do so. Every church should not just be concerned about the good news being spread where they are but helping to get the good news to places that have never heard. One way we can do that is through sending - money and missionaries and supporting those who have been sent.

To support mission work through money and people can appear at times to a church body as a losing venture. When you send people to help start a new church to reach new people it may seem like a loss. When you give away funds that could have been used locally to help globally it may seem like a loss. But once we are helping to spread the good news to the whole world, we will help to usher in the ultimate rule of God's Kingdom.

LET GOD GROW THE CHURCH

There is a principle that we seem to find in the Bible that when we seek the welfare of someone other than ourselves, that is when we are most complete. That principle applies to the church as well. Matthew 6:33 says to us to "Seek first the kingdom of God and his righteousness and all these things will be added unto you." Jesus tells his disciples and tells us that our priority should be to seek the kingdom. He over and over warns us against being wrapped up in self-preservation. We find life by losing it.

As we look at the early church in Acts, it is clear they sought the advancement of the kingdom. They were a sending church and a serving church. And Acts 2 records these words in verse 47 "And the Lord added to the church daily those who were being saved." The words that grab me are "The Lord added to the church."

Maybe that's what our focus should be on. If we focus on advancing the kingdom, then God will grow the church. If local churches focus on being a part of kingdom advancement in all three areas, God will grow their church.

At the end, maybe that's what winning is all about.

DISCUSSION QUESTIONS

1. What is one way the local body you are a part of can work toward advancing the Kingdom of God rather than seeking to simply grow itself?

2. How can you be a part of God's plan to advance the Kingdom of God where you are?

CONCLUSION

This Is the ChURch

Here is the full description we have worked through:

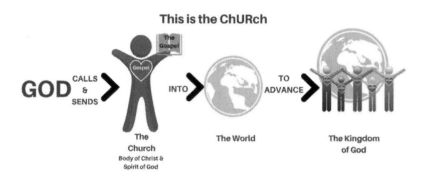

The chURch is:

• the body of Christ filled with the Spirit of God.

• motivated by the gospel and shares the gospel.

• called out of the world and sent back into the world by God.

• given the mission to advance the Kingdom of God.

PRAYER

Let me close with a prayer for each of you who have taken the time to read this.

My prayer for you is that you would see yourself in God's plan on earth and see that as a part of that plan, He wants you to be in connection with others.

My prayer is that you would have a greater appreciation for the good news of the gift of salvation. That it would free you from the heaviness of trying to make things up to God and cause you to enjoy serving Him.

My prayer is that you would allow the power of the gospel to change you, to make you more like God. It really does have power!

My prayer is that you would find who God is sending you to serve, and that you would embody the gospel to them. I pray you would live saved and sent and realize you are already equipped with everything you need including the Spirit of God.

My prayer is that you would live out the principles of God's kingdom as a servant in your community and be the visible hands and feet of Jesus in this world. I pray that you would be a part of spreading the good news so far and wide that we see God's kingdom come fully here on earth.

Finally, I pray each person would belong to a group of believers, no matter where you meet, that would live out all of these wonderful things God has called us to be as the church. I pray that if you do not have strong community, God would help you to be a part of creating it where you are.

Because, You are the ChURch!!

About the Author

Kymone Hinds, his wife and their three energetic children live in Memphis, TN. He pastors two churches, Overton Park SDA and Journey Fellowship. He also speaks and writes regularly on different life issues.

You can connect with Kymone via Twitter (@kymonehinds) or on his website at www.kymonehinds.com where he hosts a podcast and blog.

KYMONE HINDS
IDEAS TO LIFE

Made in the USA
Lexington, KY
03 August 2017